written by JODEE MCCONNAUGHHAY

illustrated by JILL DUBIN

For Anna, who loves Jesus. Always trust him! Love, Mom

Text © 1999 JoDee McConnaughhay. © 1999, 2006 Standard Publishing,
Cincinnati, Ohio. A division of Standex International Corporation.
All rights reserved.
Printed in the United States of America.
Series design: Robert Glover. Cover and interior design: Steve Clark.
All Scripture quotations, unless otherwise indicated, are taken from
the Holy Bible, *New Living Translation*, copyright © 1996.
Used by permission of Tyndale House Publishers, Inc., Wheaton, Illinois 60189.
All rights reserved.

ISBN 0-7847-1830-X

12 11 10 09 08 07 06   9 8 7 6 5 4 3 2 1

Standard®
PUBLISHING
Bringing The Word to Life

Cincinnati, Ohio

Anna was tucked snugly in her bed.

She was sleepy,

but her eyes were wide open.

"Daddy!" Anna cried,

as she ducked under her soft quilt.

Daddy came quickly into the room.

"What's wrong?" he asked.

"I'm afraid," Anna said.

Daddy said, "When I'm afraid I always say,

'The Lord is my helper, so I will not be afraid.'"

Then Daddy and Anna said the verse together.

"'The Lord is my helper, so I will not be afraid.'"

Anna hugged her knees to her chest.

"I like it," she said, "but how does it help?"

"It reminds us that God is always with us,"
Daddy said.
"And with such a big, strong helper,
we don't need to stay afraid."

"So," Daddy asked, "what will you say
when you're afraid in your bed?"
"'The Lord is my helper,
so I will not be afraid,'" Anna said.

"And when you see the doctor
because you are sick?"
"'The Lord is my helper,
so I will not be afraid,'"
Anna said.

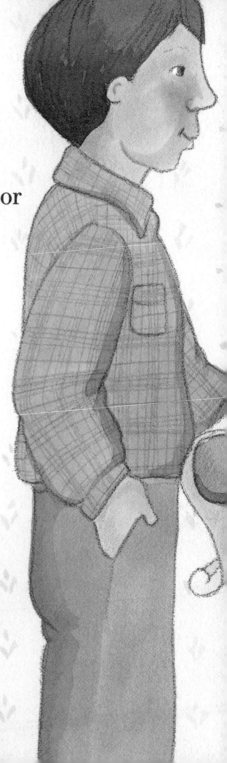

"And when Bethany's big dog runs over to play?"

"'The Lord is my helper,

so I will not be afraid,'" Anna said.

"But what if the thunder is crashing,

and lightning is flashing,

outside your window?

What will you say then, my dear?"

Anna snuggled in her bed and said,

"'The Lord is my helper, so I will not be afraid.'"

Daddy smiled, kissed Anna's cheek,

and stepped softly from the room.

Tucked snugly in her bed,

Anna knew—God was there, too.

So she smiled, closed her sleepy eyes,

and said, "'The Lord is my helper,

so I . . . will . . . not . . . be . . . afraid.'"